Never Pay for $tuff Again

STEVEN MANN

Never Pay for $tuff Again

Copyright © 2012 by Steven Mann

Trademarks

Warning and Disclaimer

About the Author

Steve Mann was born and raised in Philadelphia, Pennsylvania, where he still resides. He is an Enterprise Application Engineer for Morgan Lewis and has more than 18 years of professional experience. Steve graduated Drexel University in 1993. He has authored and co-authored several books related to collaboration technology, consulting, and saving money.

Steve's blog site can be found at:
www.SteveTheManMann.com

This page intentionally left blank

Introduction

This book presents a way of thinking about the future in regards to future expenses. While it is key to have retirement funds to live off while not working anymore, it is also key to reduce expenses so your money lasts longer. After seeing investments dwindle in the stock market, I began thinking of other ways to invest in my future. The premise being if you never had to pay for something anymore, your future expenses could be reduced.

Premise

The overall goal is to accumulate things that you use throughout your life and have enough of those things such that you never have to purchase those items ever again. It reduces your future expenses greatly because a) you don't have to pay for those items in the future and b) with inflation, the prices of those items will most likely rise. So you are saving in two ways.

Some may say this is impossible but it is actually not. The key for these items is that they must have certain attributes as follows:

- Will most likely rise in cost
- Small enough to store without incurring storage fees
- Usage is finite and can be calculated
- Cost is small
- Does not expire or go bad
- Generally can't get ruined

So you wouldn't stock up on furniture or cars or anything large and costly. You also wouldn't stock up on things that would eventually go bad or could get ruined. But what could you stock up on for future use?

Postage Stamps

The first thing I thought of was postage stamps. Once the U.S. Postal Service issued their Forever stamps, this became a key idea. The Forever stamps may be purchased at the current postage rate but if the standard letter rate increases, the stamps are still good.

This is perfect! Stamps are small and can be stored very easily. They are cheap (currently 44 cents in the US) and since I pay most of my bills online now, their usage is finite and can be calculated.

I started stocking up on postage stamps several years ago, so I already had a jump start. So now I need to figure how many I need to never pay for stamps again. Let's do some math.

Now that I pay my bills online I rarely need to mail any standard letters. Therefore I can easily say that I may only need to use about two stamps per month for random letters. Figure out what your usage is per month.

(stamps per month) X (12 months) = usage per year

Since I am saying I only use 2 stamps per month that is only 24 stamps per year. This doesn't include holiday stamps but that is next.

Therefore if I live until I am 80 years old, I have 39 years left to mail letters. For round numbers I will use 40 years. Figure out how many years you will need stamps.

(stamps per year) X (# of years) = total number of stamps

For me, I only need 864 stamps. They come in books of twenty. So therefore I need 44 books of stamps. Since this is a reasonable amount I can purchase a few books each month. So far I have about 24 books so I only need 20 more. They all fit in a desk drawer and do not take up space. Perfect!

I then need about 1 book each year for holiday cards so that is not too bad. This is separate since they have Forever holiday stamps that don't have the Liberty Bell on them. They also have party stamps that are available as Forever as well. I will stock up on these also.

UPDATE: From the time I originally wrote this (which was a few months ago), I don't think I used a single stamp. I am really thinking that I may only use 1 stamp per month on average. The price of stamps are going up in the U.S. again so I bought 100 more stamps. That's 5 more books so I have about 30 books total now. I think I have enough for the rest of my life!!!

Check Books

The next thing I am stocking up on is check books. I need to purchase check books from my credit union. Since I am paying bills online I rarely need to write checks. My wife and I write checks for school items and such (e.g. school trips, lunch program, pictures, etc.). Again, only about two or three checks a month. Once my kids are all out of high school (in about 5 years), I probably won't need to write as many per month.

Printing costs will rise and I have seen the check book prices go up over the past twenty years of my check writing life. I usually purchase 4 boxes at a time. The last time I purchased 4 boxes was May 6th of 2010 and I have about 2 1/2 boxes still left (as of January 2012).

Yes they take up more room than stamps but I can usually consolidate those 4 boxes into 3 since they come with register books and other things that I don't need or use.

So since I only need about 36 checks per year, I figure over the next forty years I'll need about 1440 checks. I believe I get 100 checks in each box so that would mean I need about 14 more boxes. Not bad!

Since I know I will write less checks once my kids are out of high school, I can probably get way with 12 more boxes. I can consolidate these into 9 boxes so they won't take up that much space.

UPDATE: I did a Google search and found www.extravaluechecks.com. They are very cheap and who cares what the checks look like. It is not like I am happy writing a check - that means I am giving away money. I was able to order 8 boxes for a little under $40. With the shipping charges it was around $56. I ordered the singles this time as having the duplicate hardly ever comes in handy anymore - since I don't really write checks anyway. These boxes contain 126 checks each. I have a little over 350 checks on hand and those eight boxes will provide 1008 more. So that's 1358 checks. That may just about do it!

Light Bulbs

I finally have most of my light bulbs switched over to CFL to save energy. I had a few blow out over the past 5 years but for the most part they have been lasting pretty long. But now there are LED light bulbs that are expected to last anywhere from 22-50 years depending on usage. That is awesome!

The LED bulbs save so much energy. I bought a few for my bathroom vanity and they only use 2 watts each. These are the globe kind.

I bought a single LED bulb to test it in other light fixtures. This bulb is 4 watts and is expected to last 22 years. On the box it stated that it only costs $0.90 to run each year. Excellent!

The only problem is that these LED bulbs are currently expensive! I purchased several for $15 USD each. That's a lot for a bulb but even if it lasts 10 years it is paying for itself by saving energy and lasting longer.

Just like the CFL bulbs, I am sure the LED bulbs will come down in price eventually. However, I am anxious to start replacing some of my CFLs with LEDs to reduce my electric bill once again.

So if I purchase enough bulbs now, I can stock up for when they blow out. I always have spare bulbs stored anyway so this won't take up too much more space. If I purchase enough now, I may never need to purchase a single light bulb ever again!

UPDATE: I stopped into Lowe's several times and found a certain LED bulb reduced in price. First it was $15 as stated in the original writing above. The next time I went to the store it was reduced to $11-something – great; I bought a handful. The second time after that they were down to a special $9-something – what? Similar bulbs were standing around $20. I found nothing wrong with the reduced ones. They produce nice bright white light and run 7 watts. So I replaced some of my CFLs running 13 watts with these.

Trash Bags

What a great product to sell - something you buy to throw out and need to buy again. Because they are plastic and are not going to the recycling plant (in some areas), I try to not to use too many trash bags each week.

I use the white kitchen size (13 gal) in the bathrooms and bedrooms while using the larger 33 gal black bags in the kitchen. I use one for the trash can and one for the recycling can (only so I can easily take out the recycling). I usually reuse the empty recycling bag for the outside trash can in front of the house.

I use about three large black bags and three white bags each week. I try to consolidate the trash and reuse any liners that are messy or smelly. This is also something that I will use less of once the kids are grown and out of the house. So there will be less trash and less trash cans to line with bags.

Since trash bag usage is a finite number that can be calculated, I really want to stock up on them. The prices will probably go up over the next 40 years. You can purchase them in bulk boxes, which I do for normal usage, at the many wholesale clubs around town (e.g. BJs, Costco, Sam's Club, etc.). The boxes are rectangular and can be stacked nicely somewhere.

Right now it seems I need 1-2 boxes of each kind per year. That would be a lot to stock up on for another 40 years. Eventually, I'll probably be down to only a half of one box of each kind per year which is more manageable. The boxes will take up some space so I need to be careful about that as well. If I bought 10 boxes of each kind today, that may not cover the rest of my life. I'll need to think about this and revisit.

Razor Blades

I always need razor blades for my utility knifes and such. They come in handy for clean cutting of various materials. Since they are small and cheap, they become a good candidate for stocking up and never having to buy again. I am thinking if I bought a 100 pack of blades, I should be good. This may be a nice quick hit.

UPDATE: I found a package of razors that came with two containers of 75 each for a total of 150 razors. The package was $12-something. I think that should do it!

Nails and Screws

When I was heavy into home improvement items, I went through plenty of nails and screws. Now, I just need them here and there to hang pictures or decorations. I have several different kinds in stock at the moment. They are small and the boxes are stackable. I am thinking maybe a few bucks for a few more boxes and I would be set - never needing to purchase nails or screws ever again.

Dress Shirts

Looking back at some pictures, I realized that I have had some dress shirts for as many as 8 years and still going strong. I have about 20-30 shirts in my current wardrobe but that includes backup shirts (shirts I don't like to wear but will if all the others are at the cleaners or in the laundry) and what I call "fancy shirts" (the more expensive dress shirts that I wear with suits or sport jacket outfits).

I do notice some wear on certain shirts. My wife used to wash them at home but now we take them to the cleaners. Even the dry cleaning exposes some wear as I have noticed in the older shirts.

From this I can see which ones seem to hold up and which ones are degrading each month. I noticed that the sateen shirts can get a worn look and some appear to have "fuzzies" in the material. I will probably have to get rid of these sooner than later. On the other hand, I can tell which shirts are standing up to the wear and dry cleaning.

My "fancy" shirts seem to do the best but are more expensive. I also don't wear them as often so I can't say for sure that these are holding up better. However, I can tell the difference in quality and therefore may make the investment to purchase a handful more.

I am thinking maybe 20 more shirts and I may be good. I do, however, need new dress pants first so it may be awhile before I stock up on new shirts.

Car Washes

Most car washes offer books of coupons for future usage. The more you buy, the cheaper the wash. I do purchase these books, however, eventually I would like to purchase an insane amount such that I have enough for a lifetime.

My only problem is that the establishment I currently frequent and own prepaid washes is a one-of-a-kind family-owned business. So there is risk that any prepaid washes could last longer than the business.

There are, however, car wash brands that are more established and have multiple locations. These companies offer prepaid books as well. It would probably less risky to purchase these books than at a local service center.

So I can purchase several books at the local car wash and then purchase the rest from the more established service brand. The coupon books are easy to store and won't take up much room. They are, however, not as cheap as stamps, so I'll put this on my list but may need to save up to achieve the lifetime purchase.

Envelopes

Duh! I can't believe it took so long to think of envelopes. These are similar usage to postage stamps and checks. I did purchase a large-count box of small envelopes and large business envelopes in which I still have plenty. I think the small envelopes cost me more than the larger ones – go figure.

The boxes are in a large drawer in my office with a bunch of crap on top so I really can't see how many are left. We usually just stick our hands in there and pull out a few.

The boxes take up some room since they are the large count (500 in each I believe) but I am thinking another box of each kind and I should be good.

Socks and Underwear

Yes socks and underwear will get worn out but what if you stocked up on several packages worth? If you have room in your drawers or closet, it may not be a bad idea.

I am not sure about socks since my kids take all the good ones from the wash but I know I have some underwear from at least 5-7 years ago. They are on their way out but even the newest pairs are at least 4-5 years old.

Since I lost a lot of weight, I can probably go a few sizes smaller. Maybe I'll buy 10 packs or something and see what happens. I'll store probably 5-7 of those packs.

Things That May Not Be Good

I wish there were more things because, believe me, I don't like paying for the same crap over and over again and I am sure you don't enjoy it as well.

Below is a listing of things that you may want to stock up on here and there but probably can't buy enough to last the rest of your life.

Item	Reasons
Paper towels, toilet paper, tissues, napkins	Take up space Could get ruined if wet Potential fire hazard
Canned goods	Take up space Eventually won't be good
Frozen foods and meats	Take up space Eventually won't be good
Computers	Outdated in 1-2 years Sometimes outdated as soon as you set it up
TVs	Outdated in 1-2 years Will they ever stop getting better??

Readers' Ideas

If you have any more ideas on items that fit the "never buy again" model, send them to steve@stevethemanmann.com

If your idea is selected, it will be published in the next edition of this guide providing you full credit. Plus I'll send you an Amazon gift card based on the sales of the edition(s) your entry appears.

Saving Time and Money

I have other great ideas on how to save time and money on anything and everything you do in life. I will be writing a guide book on this topic so stayed tuned and be on the lookout for my next money-saving guide.